I0804596

rockschool®

Piano

US Level 2 (UK Grade 2)

Performance pieces, technical exercises, supporting tests and in-depth guidance for Rockschool assessments

All accompanying and supporting audio can be downloaded from: *www.rslawards.com/downloads*

Input the following code when prompted: **43QVCEMJBZ**

For more information, turn to page 5

www.rslawards.com

Acknowledgements

Published by Rockschool Ltd. © 2019 & 2020
Catalogue Number: RSK200091US
ISBN: 978-1-78936-167-4
Initial US Release | Errata details can be found at *www.rslawards.com/errata*

SYLLABUS
Syllabus designed and written by Jono Harrison
Syllabus Director: Tim Bennett-Hart
Syllabus consultants: Gary Sanctuary, Chris Stanbury, Simon Troup and Jennie Troup
Hit Tune arrangements by Jono Harrison and Gary Sanctuary
Supporting Tests written by Jono Harrison, Chris Stanbury, Nik Preston and Ash Preston
Syllabus advisors: Tim Bennett-Hart, Brian Ashworth, Stuart Slater, Peter Huntington, Bruce Darlington, Simon Troup and Jennie Troup

PUBLISHING
Proof reading of arrangements by Sharon Kelly, Simon Troup, Jennie Troup and Jono Harrison
Music engraving and book layout by Simon and Jennie Troup of Digital Music Art
Fact files written and edited by Abbie Thomas
Notes written by Roland Perrin
Proof reading and copy editing by Gemma Bull, Jono Harrison and Jennie Troup
Cover design by Philip Millard of Rather Nice Design
Cover photograph: © Nomad_Soul (Shutterstock)

AUDIO
Produced by Jono Harrison
Engineered by Jono Harrison, Gary Sanctuary, Tim Bennett-Hart, Pete Riley, Richard Brook, Rory Harvey and Andy Robertson
Assisted by Paul Pritchard at Abbey Road
Recorded at Dock Street Studios, The Dairy and Abbey Road
Mixed by Patrick Phillips
Mastered by Francis Gorini

Supporting Tests recorded by Chris Stanbury and Jono Harrison

MUSICIANS
Piano and Keyboards: Jono Harrison, Gary Sanctuary, Ross Stanley & Tania Ilyashova
Drums & Percussion: Pete Riley and Richard Brook
Bass & Synth Bass: Andy Robertson
Guitars: Rory Harvey, Nat Martin and Jono Harrison
Saxophone: Jonathan Griffiths
Trombone: Tom George White and Norton York
Trumpet: Nick Mead and John Simpson
Lead and Backing Vocals: Glen Harvey & Katie Hector
Additional Programming: Jono Harrison

DISTRIBUTION
Exclusive Distributors: Hal Leonard

CONTACTING ROCKSCHOOL
www.rslawards.com
Telephone: +44 (0)345 460 4747
Email: *info@rslawards.com*

EXECUTIVE PRODUCERS
John Simpson, Norton York

Awarding the Contemporary Arts

Table of Contents

Welcome to Rockschool Piano Level/Grade 2

Welcome to Rockschool's Piano syllabus 2019. This syllabus is designed to support pianists in their progression from Debut to Level/Grade 8, through an engaging and rigorous pathway covering all the genres, stylistic elements, techniques and musical skills required for success as a contemporary pianist.

Piano Assessments

At each level/grade you have the option of taking one of two different types of assessment:

- Level/**Grade Assessment**
  A Level/Grade Assessment is a mixture of music performances, technical work and tests. You are required to prepare three pieces (two of which may be Free Choice Pieces) and the contents of the Technical Exercise section. This accounts for 75% of the assessment marks. The other 25% consists of: either a Sight Reading or an Improvisation & Interpretation test (10%), two Ear Tests (10%), and finally you will be asked five General Musicianship Questions (5%). The pass mark is 60%.

- **Performance Certificate**
  A Performance Certificate is equivalent to a Level/Grade Assessment, but in a Performance Certificate you are required to perform five pieces. A maximum of three of these can be Free Choice Pieces. Each song is marked out of 20 and the pass mark is 60%.

All elements required to participate in a Rockschool assessment can be found in the level/grade book. These are as follows:

- **Assessment Pieces**
  The 2019 syllabus comprises six 'hit tune' arrangements, benchmarked and devised so as to equip contemporary pianists with industry-relevant skills in any performance environment. These fall into three categories:

  Melody & Accompaniment
  These arrangements are performed to full band backing tracks, with the piano performing both melody and accompaniment

  Solo Piano Arrangement
  These are full solo piano arrangements, performed without backing tracks

  Vocal Accompaniment
  These arrangements cover the skills required of contemporary pianists in ensemble environments, be they on the stage or in the studio. The backing tracks feature vocalists, and the piano parts are reflective of what session pianists would perform live or on mainstream commercial recordings

  Each 'hit tune' arrangement is preceded by a Fact File, giving surrounding context to the piece and the original performers/recording artists.

  Furthermore, at the end of each arrangement you will find notes giving additional supportive context to get the most out of the pieces.

- **Technical Exercises**
  There are either three or four groups of technical exercise, depending on the level/grade:

  Debut–Level/Grade 8:
  Group A: Scales
  Group B: Arpeggios/Broken Chords
  Group C: Chord Voicings

  Levels/Grades 4–8 only:
  Group D: Technical Study

- **Supporting Tests**
  There are three types of unprepared supporting tests in the assessment:

  1. The first type can be one of two options (this is the *candidate's* choice):

     Either:
     Sight Reading tests, developing the musician's ability to read and perform previously unseen material;

     or:
     Improvisation & Interpretation tests, developing the musician's ability to develop previously unseen material in a stylistic way and perform improvised passages of melody. The book contains examples of both types of test – equivalent 'unseen' examples will be provided for the assessment

  2. **Ear Tests**
     Debut–Level/Grade 3: feature Melodic Recall and Chord Recognition
     Levels/Grades 4–8: feature Melodic Recall and Harmonic Recall

  3. **General Musicianship Questions (GMQs)**, which you will be asked by the assessor at the end of each assessment

General Information

You will find information on assessment procedures, including online assessment entry, marking schemes, information on Free Choice Pieces and improvisation requirements for each level/grade.

Audio

In addition to the level/grade book, we have also provided audio in the form of backing tracks (minus piano) and full tracks (including piano) for all 'hit tune' arrangements, technical exercises and supporting tests (where applicable). We have provided professional performance recordings of all solo piano pieces in the syllabus. This audio can be downloaded from RSL directly at *www.rslawards.com/downloads*

You will need to input this code when prompted: **43QVCEMJBZ**

The audio files are supplied in MP3 format. Once downloaded you will be able to play them on any compatible device.

Further Information

You can find further details about Rockschool's Contemporary Piano syllabus by downloading the syllabus guide from our website: *www.rslawards.com*

All candidates should download and read the accompanying syllabus guide when using this level/grade book.

Performance and Technical Guidance

Fingering
Any fingering annotation is given as a guide only.

Interpretation
Notation should be performed exactly as written, except where there are performance indications to ad. lib, improvise, develop, etc. In these instances, the candidate will be marked on their ability to interpret the music in a stylistically appropriate way, commensurate with the level.

Adaptation
A small degree of adaptation is allowed where, for example, hand stretches do not facilitate the required notated parts. Marks may be deducted if adaptation results in over-simplification of the notation. If in doubt you can submit any adaptation enquiries to *info@rslawards.com*

Articulation & Dynamics
Where articulation and dynamics are marked on the notation, they should be followed. Where it is open to interpretation, the candidate is free to take their own approach.

Pedalling
The candidate may use the pedal freely at any level/grade, but it should be applied judiciously as marks may be deducted for any over usage resulting in an unclear tone. In addition, where pedalling is written into (or out of) the notation, this should be observed.

Chord Symbols
Most hit tune arrangements have chord symbols written above the notation. This is purely for guidance, and to assist the candidate and teacher.

Thinking Out Loud

SONG TITLE: THINKING OUT LOUD
ALBUM: X
LABEL: ASYLUM / ATLANTIC
GENRE: BLUE EYED SOUL / POP

WRITTEN BY: ED SHEERAN, AMY WADGE AND JULIAN WILLIAMS
PRODUCED BY: JAKE GOSLING

US CHART PEAK: 2

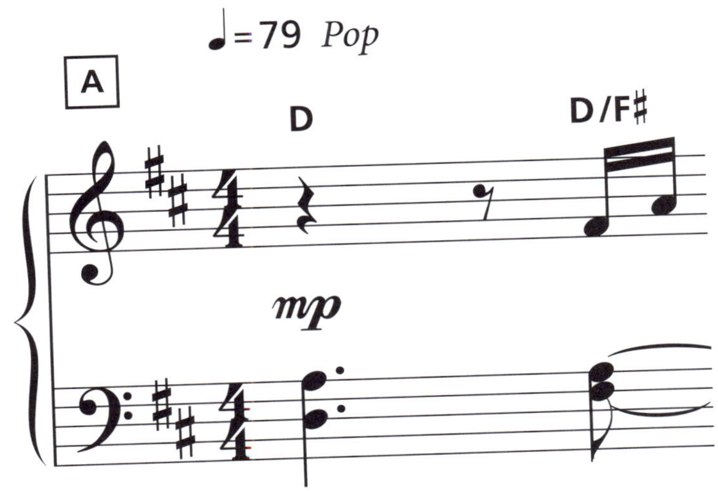

'Thinking Out Loud' was released as a single in September 2014 and reached the no.2 spot on the Billboard Hot 100 subsequently spending a year in the Top Forty. It reached no.1 in many countries across the world and by 2015 it had reached half a billion streams on Spotify and over 2 billion views on YouTube. The song won two Grammy Awards, for Best Pop Solo Performance and Song Of The Year respectively.

'Thinking Out Loud' was written in partnership with long-time collaborator Amy Wadge, who Sheeran has worked with since 2007. They also collaborated on the 2017 single 'Shape Of You', a massive worldwide success. 'Thinking Out Loud' is a romantic ballad and its lyrics reflect the feeling of getting older and how love and fidelity are impacted by it. Sheeran has defined the song as a 'walking down the aisle song'. The song's similarities with Marvin Gaye's 'Let's Get It On' brought claims of plagiarism that were later withdrawn. 'Thinking Out Loud' has sold in excess of 10 million copies worldwide.

Ed Sheeran's meteoric rise to fame has been the result of a highly productive work ethic. He performs relentlessly to this day, as a solo acoustic artist, to thousands of fans worldwide.

His 2017 album '÷' had, at one time, a record 10 singles in the UK Singles Chart

Sheeran was born in West Yorkshire in 1991 and raised in Suffolk. He dropped out of school aged 16 to pursue a career in music and moved to London. His independent releases caught the attention of Elton John and Jamie Foxx, and he signed to Asylum records in 2011. He is one of today's most popular and commercially successful artists.

Sheeran is an outspoken artist, not afraid of making his political and social views known, and he remains an accessible and down to earth character. He is an actor, and had cameos in *Game of Thrones*, *Home and Away* and *The Simpsons*.

With only three albums to his name to date, Ed Sheeran has already had an immensely successful career.

Thinking Out Loud

Ed Sheeran

B
Em7 A D Em7
[17]
A Em7 A Bm
[20]
Em7 A
[23]
C
D D/F♯ G A7 D D/F♯
mf
3
[25]
G A7 D D/F♯ G A7
3 3 3
[28]
D D/F♯ G A7
[31]
Bm A G D/F♯ Em7 A D
[33]

Notes

In section A, one of the biggest challenges is to maintain the pulse where the music is sustained across a beat. In the opening eight measures of the piece, each two-measure melodic phrase starts consistently on the *and* of the second beat. Similarly, as the left hand chord is tied across to beat three, it is up to the performer to keep a strict quarter-note internal pulse to make sure the tempo stays steady.

Be careful not to let the left hand chords overwhelm the right-hand melody line. While they help provide the harmony and reinforce the syncopated groove, sections A and B should be performed with a light touch and remaining moderately quiet throughout.

While the rests between the phrases in the right-hand melody mirror those phrases sung by the vocalist, there are three key points in the piece where both hands have simultaneous rests (measures 16, 18 and 22). Be sure to observe these rests in order to create the contrast provided by these brief moments of silence.

In measure 24, note that there is a *crescendo* leading into section C. Be careful to moderate this increase in volume to avoid changing the light open character, while allowing the melody to sing out above the left hand chords.

Students should take notice of the triplets in measures 26, 28 and 30. These measures are best practised in isolation to ensure they understand the rhythm pattern of the melody line in relation to the pulse. One approach would be to focus solely on the rhythm by tapping out a steady quarter-note pulse with the left hand while tapping out the rhythm pattern with their right hand to understand how it fits across the four beats. It may be beneficial to practise this slowly, before bringing up to tempo.

This Is Me

SONG TITLE: 'THIS IS ME'
ALBUM: THE GREATEST SHOWMAN: ORIGINAL MOTION PICTURE SOUNDTRACK
RELEASED: 2017
LABEL: ATLANTIC
GENRE: POP
WRITTEN BY: BENJ PASEK/JUSTIN PAUL
PRODUCED BY: GREG WELLS/JUSTIN PAUL/ ADAM GUBMAN/ ALEX LACAMOIRE
US CHART PEAK: 58

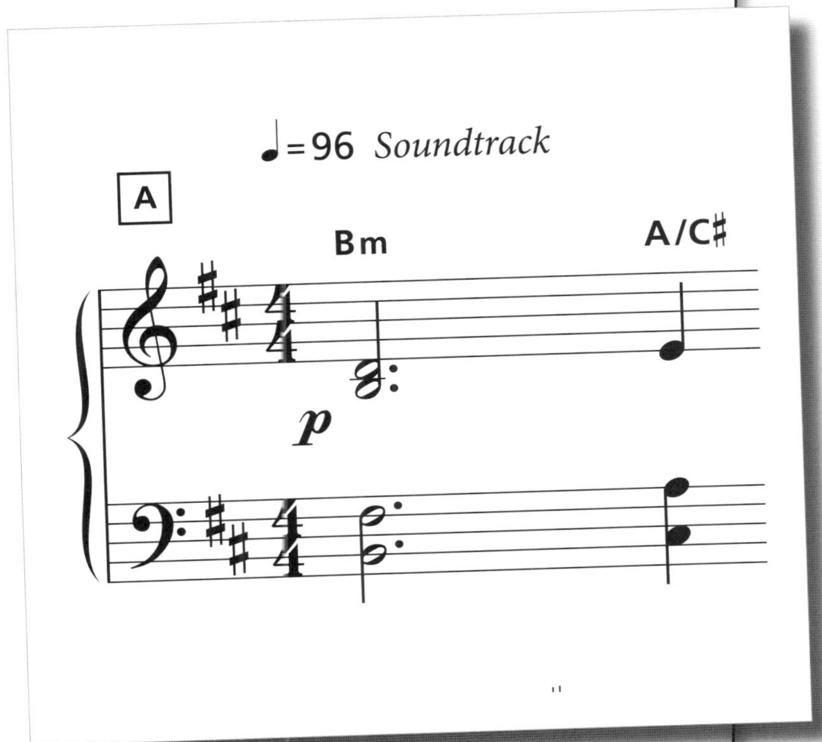

'This Is Me' is a pop song with an anthemic feel, written for the 2017 musical film release 'The Greatest Showman'. The song was originally released as a promotional tool for the film on October 26th 2017 and was later released as the official lead single for the soundtrack on December 8th of the same year. Following the film's official release 'This Is Me' achieved worldwide success, peaking at number 3 on the UK Singles Chart and reaching the top 10 in Australia, Malaysia and South Korea as well as the top 20 in Ireland, Belgium and New Zealand.

The lead vocal for 'This Is Me' was performed by American Broadway star Keala Settle. The actress and singer made her Broadway debut in 2011 as Shirley in 'Priscilla, Queen of the Desert'. She later went on to originate the role of Norma Valverde in 'Hands on a Hardbody' in 2013, for which she received several nominations including the Tony Award nomination for 'Best Featured Actress in a Musical'. The role also saw her receive the Theatre World Award for 'Outstanding Broadway Debut Performance'. Settle also performed as part of the cast for the 2014 Broadway revival of Les Misérables, playing the part of Madame Thenardier. Shortly before going on to achieve Box Office success with The Greatest Showman, Settle also originated the role of Becky for the 2016 Broadway debut of the musical 'Waitress'.

'The Greatest Showman' was met with mixed reviews, with many praising the performances, music and production values, while others criticised the plot and described it as shallow and artificial. Despite the mixed reviews the blockbuster did well in the Box Office, with a gross income of over $430 million worldwide, making it the 16th highest grossing film of 2017. The film received several award nominations, including the Golden Globe nominations for 'Best Motion Picture' & 'Best Actor' (Hugh Jackman), but it was 'This Is Me' that achieved the most award success. Winning the Golden Globe for 'Best Original Song', the track was also nominated for the same award at the 2017 Oscars and has been nominated for 'Best Song Written for Visual Media' at the up and coming 2019 Grammys.

This Is Me

Keala Settle and The Greatest Showman Ensemble

From 'The Greatest Showman' (2017)

C
Bm A/C♯ D G Bm Asus4 A
mf
[26]
Bm A/C♯ D G Bm A
[30]
D
Gmaj7 A Bm A/C♯ D Aadd4
[34]
E
D Bm7
f
[38]
Gmaj7 A D
[42]
Bm7 Gsus2 A
[46]

Notes

'This Is Me' features distinct lifts in dynamic and groove from one section to the next, enforcing the theme of positivity and strength running through the lyrics. The first part of this song (measures 1 to 13) have a quiet and direct simplicity, and this hymn-like section will be most effective when played with clear and precise articulation. Students should avoid the temptation to over-use the pedal, which could adversely affect the clarity between the chords. As both the treble and bass clef often follow the same rhythmic pattern, students should listen carefully to their timing to ensure that the left and right hands sound precisely together at these points, paying careful attention to the balance of every note in each chord. At measure 9, there is a slight lift to *mezzo piano* dynamic, as we anticipate the first chorus at measure 14 (section B).

Care is needed to avoid inadvertently increasing the volume when the left hand moves to a quarter-note pattern in measures 20 to 23. Furthermore, some students might find the right hand syncopations in measures 20 and 22 are challenging. If so, measure 20 can be practised by playing it as a 'loop' with the ties omitted – the notes 'E' and 'G' being repeated. Once this has been mastered at the correct tempo, the ties can be included.

Sections C and D build on the previous two sections and should be performed moderately loudly. Be careful not to raise the volume too much at this point in the piece to allow room for a good contrast with the following louder section. While this should feel like a sense of progression and development, it is important to maintain the original dignified and calm character of the previous sections.

The second part of the song, at measure 38, breaks out into a defiant marching groove. This needs to be played *forte*. Students should ensure that this change provides a real sense of contrast – there should be no hint of a *crescendo* in the measures leading up to it.

One of the principal challenges of this piece is to keep a sense of forward motion and development while avoiding a gradual drift of tempo. Students could benefit from playing alongside a metronome click at a slower tempo at first, to help prepare for playing to the backing track.

Finally the piano part finished on an unresolved 'A' chord – this is because the piece is actually finished by the singer, with the rest of the ensemble leaving a rest at the end of the measure for full impact.

The Pink Panther Theme

SONG TITLE: 'THE PINK PANTHER THEME'
ALBUM: THE PINK PANTHER
RELEASED: 1963
LABEL: RCA VICTOR
GENRE: JAZZ
WRITTEN BY: HENRY MANCINI
PRODUCED BY: JOE REISMAN
US CHART PEAK: 8

'The Pink Panther Theme' was composed by Henry Mancini for the release of the original 1963 film The Pink Panther. The piece was subsequently nominated for 'Best Score' at the 1964 Academy Awards, losing out only to the Sherman Brothers' iconic Mary Poppins score. Mancini's composition was included in the film's soundtrack 'The Pink Panther' and was actually released as a single in the US, where it peaked at the impressive position of number 8.

The score was composed carefully with animation of the soon to be famous character in mind. Mancini actually gave the animators a tempo before they set to work, one which he knew would allow him to carefully sync movement such as striking motions to the score. On receiving the animation, Mancini was pleased to find that the movement was very much workable and he continued to write around the character's motion. This delivers a classic but comical animation, one which became iconic to viewers and remains so to this day.

Henry Mancini was an American composer, conductor and arranger, remembered most prominently for his work in film and television scoring. Having written his first film score in 1951 for Ted Tatzlaff's film noir release 'Under the Gun', Mancini went on to score until his sad passing in 1994. At the time of his death the composer was writing the score for the stage adaption of 'Victor Victoria', a musical comedy which he wrote the original film score for in 1982, but sadly he never survived to see it performed.

Throughout his career Mancini was most certainly revered as an influential composer and arranger. Before passing away in 1994 he was awarded 19 Grammy awards for his work in film and television composition, and in 1995 he received a posthumous Lifetime Achievement Grammy Award. Although his Academy award nomination for 'The Pink Panther Theme' didn't produce a win, the composer was awarded four Academy Awards throughout his career. In 1961 he was awarded two Oscars for his work on the classic 'Breakfast at Tiffany's', one being for Best Original Song ('Moonriver') and the other being for Best Dramatic Scoring of a Dramatic or Comedy Picture. He also won Best Song in 1962 for his composition 'Days of Wine and Roses' written for the film of the same name, and lastly Best Original Score for 'Victor Victoria' in 1982.

The Pink Panther Theme

Henry Mancini

From 'The Pink Panther' (1963)

2.
mf
[14]
3
mp
[16]
3
[18]
p
[20]
f
[22]
[24]

Notes

This song has a jazzy feel and a sense that there is much more behind the music than first appears. The notes appear fairly simple but, if they are played with precision and attention to the details of articulation, the piece will sound *cool*.

For practice purposes, students could be encouraged to count a medium slow 'one, two, three, four' and, at the same time, click their fingers or clap their hands on the second and fourth beats. Once the tempo and feel have been set in this way, it is important to maintain a steady pulse throughout.

Students need to be very precise in observing the rests in the left-hand part. In this song, the left hand imitates a double bass. Note the *staccato* quarter-note at the start of measure 15. While there is a small *crescendo* leading up to this left-hand *staccato* note, be careful not to over emphasise this note as an accented note. Instead, save the peak moment for the accented chord on the final beat of measure 23.

For full effect, students should observe the *diminuendo* in measure 19, followed by playing measures 20 to 22 right back down to *piano*. The *forte* at the end will truly startle listeners.

Make sure the last two measures are played for the correct length.

Feeling Good

SONG TITLE: 'FEELING GOOD'
ALBUM: I PUT A SPELL ON YOU
RELEASED: 1965
LABEL: PHILIPS/MERCURY
GENRE: JAZZ/BLUES
WRITTEN BY: LESLIE BRICUSSE/ ANTHONY NEWLEY
PRODUCED BY: HAL MOONEY
US CHART PEAK: N/A

The song 'Feeling Good' was originally written for the musical 'The Roar of the Greasepaint – The Smell of the Crowd', by British composers Anthony Newley and Leslie Bricusse. It was first performed on stage in 1964 by Cy Grant on the shows first UK tour, before Gilbert Price went on to perform it in 1965 with the original Broadway cast. 'Feeling Good' has been covered by a huge number of inspiring artists from many different genres, but Nina Simone was the first artist to cover and release the hit as a single in 1965.

Nina Simone recorded her adaption of the song for her 1965 album I Put A Spell On You - a beautiful and complex jazz rendition – putting her own stamp on the otherwise underwhelming showtune. Although the song wasn't originally released as a single, it was later released in 1994 after becoming hugely popular for having featured in a British TV advert for Volkswagen. The song made it to number 40 in the UK Singles chart and became a prominent inspiration with many artists going on to cover the song in the coming decades.

British Rock band Muse released their version of 'Feeling Good' in 2001 on their album second studio album *Origin of Symmetry*. They were praised for their guitar driven rock version of the classic, with 'Total Guitar' ranking it the 5th best cover song ever. Michael Bublé's 2005 rendition of 'Feeling Good' was the lead single for his album *It's Time*. With a big band feel it's certainly closer to Simone's 1965 recording than that of Muse's rock anthem. In 2015 American singer, songwriter and rapper Lauryn Hill released an entire album dedicated to Nina Simone, entitled *Nina Revisited: A Tribute to Nina Simone*. On the album she featured her adaption of 'Feeling Good', paying homage to the artist that so heavily influenced her style and love for music.

Nina Simone is cited by countless seminal artists as an inspiration, including Elton John, Aretha Franklin, David Bowie, Janis Joplin, Cat Stevens, Adele, John Legend and so many more. A prominent figure in the Civil Rights Movement, she inspired thousands with not only her music but also her passion for freedom and equality. In 2000 she received a Grammy Hall of Fame award and in 2018 she was (at last) rightly inducted into the Rock and Roll Hall of Fame.

Feeling Good

Nina Simone

Trumpet Solo
Gm
Gm/F
E♭maj7
D7
Gm
Gm/F
mf
[12]
E♭maj7
D7
Gm
Gm/F
Em7♭5
E♭
[15]
Gm/D
Gm/C
B♭
Am7♭9♭5
Cm
D7
f
[18]
p
[21]
pp
[23]

Notes

In this blues/jazz song, it is essential to keep a strict feeling for the twelve eighth-note beats in each measure.

The melody in measures 1 to 10 should be articulated as much like a singer as possible, maintaining right hand *legato* whilst bringing out the melody above the left hand. Make sure the left hand part is a little quieter than the right, allowing the melody to project clearly.

Note how the music starts in a quiet, brooding way. The short *crescendo* into *forte* in measure 9 then leads into a confident and bluesy two-measure bridge which, in turn, leads into the trumpet solo at measure 12. While the trumpet solo accompaniment should be performed a little quieter than the previous two measures, this section should maintain the established confident and relaxed character of the piece. Note that while the right hand part plays continuous *staccato* eighth-notes throughout the trumpet solo, the left-hand eighth notes should feel a little heavier, while still accurately observing the rests.Another short *crescendo* to *forte* in measure 20 brings this section to a dramatic end.

The sudden drop back down to *piano* in measure 21 should provide enough of a dramatic contrast of volume to the previous measure while reserving some room to be able to execute a controlled *diminuendo* through measures 23 to 25 to a whisper of *pianissimo* in the final measure.

All these contrasts need to be carefully performed, strictly following the dynamic markings in the notation.

SONG TITLE: 'ROAR'
ALBUM: PRISM
RELEASED: 2013
LABEL: CAPITOL
GENRE: POP
WRITTEN BY: KATY PERRY/LUKASZ GOTTWALD/MAX MARTIN/ BONNIE MCKEE/HENRY WALTER
PRODUCED BY: DR LUKE/MAX MARTIN/ CIRKUT
US CHART PEAK: 1

'Roar' was a smash hit for American multimillion selling artist Katy Perry. Released as the lead single from her fourth studio album *Prism (2013),* the single was a global success and topped the charts in Australia, Austria, Canada, Ireland, Israel, Lebanon, New Zealand, Slovenia, South Korea, the UK and the US. By the end of its release year the song totalled sales of over 8 million copies worldwide and is now certified Diamond in the US with over 6 million sales there alone.

'Roar' was met with mixed reviews with many feeling the lyrics were laden with clichés and delivered little new to the listener. However, many praised Perry for her 'easy pop feel' and viewed the track as a "…change of pace" for the artist. In the past it has been likened to Sarah Bareilles' song 'Brave', with many reviewers and fans feeling a co-writing credit should have been given. However, one of the song's producer's (Dr Luke) confirmed that it was in fact written and recorded before Bareilles' release. Sarah Bareilles herself claimed that the pair are good friends and that there were never any concerns between them about the similarities.

Katy Perry was born Katheryn Hudson in 1984, she released her first album (*Katy Hudson)* in 2001 under her birth name but failed to find success with the Christian Rock record. In 2008 she rose to fame as Katy Perry with the release of her second studio album *One of the Boys,* which included the hits 'I Kissed a Girl' and 'Hot 'n' Cold'. The album was quite a change from her Christian based music roots. To date, Perry has four top 40 UK albums and five number 1 UK Singles, not to mention nine chart topping singles in the US.

Although Perry is yet to win a Grammy Award, her single 'Roar' did receive two nominations at the 2013 ceremony for 'Song of the Year' and 'Best Pop Solo Performance'. Throughout her career she has won an impressive number of awards, including five American Music Awards, fourteen People's Choice Awards, a Brit award and amazingly four Guinness World Records. The music video for her single 'Roar' has over two billion views on YouTube and the track itself has sold over 8 million copies worldwide.

Roar

Katy Perry

B♭
f
Cm7
[13]
Gm7
E♭
[15]
B♭
Cm7
[17]
Gm7
E♭
[19]
B♭
Cm7
[21]
Gm7
E♭
B♭
[23]

Notes

Teachers will need to make sure that students understand how the swing notation affects the interpretation of the 16th notes. This lilting pattern helps provide a bouncy and laidback feel to the melody in both the first eight measures of the piece and then later in measures 22 and 23 .

It is important to make sure that all the rests are correctly observed, as this will enhance the singing quality of the melody and help with shaping each musical phrase effectively.

Students should pay attention to the dynamics within this piece. Although the range is quite narrowly focussed from ***mf*** to ***f***; the *crescendo* in measure 12 leading into the chorus needs to provide enough contrast between sections to help provide a sense of direction and structure to the whole arrangement.

In measures 21, 22 and 23, the *staccato* phrases need to have a spring to them. Maintaining a loose wrist action is key to good *staccato* technique. Make sure that these notes are not inadvertently accented and aim for a consistent volume across both the *legato* and *staccato* notes within these measures.

Walk On By

SONG TITLE: 'WALK ON BY'
ALBUM: MAKE WAY FOR DIONNE WARWICK
RELEASED: 1964
LABEL: SCEPTER
GENRE: R&B
WRITTEN BY: BURT BACHARACH/HAL DAVID
PRODUCED BY: BURT BACHARACH/HAL DAVID
US CHART PEAK: 6

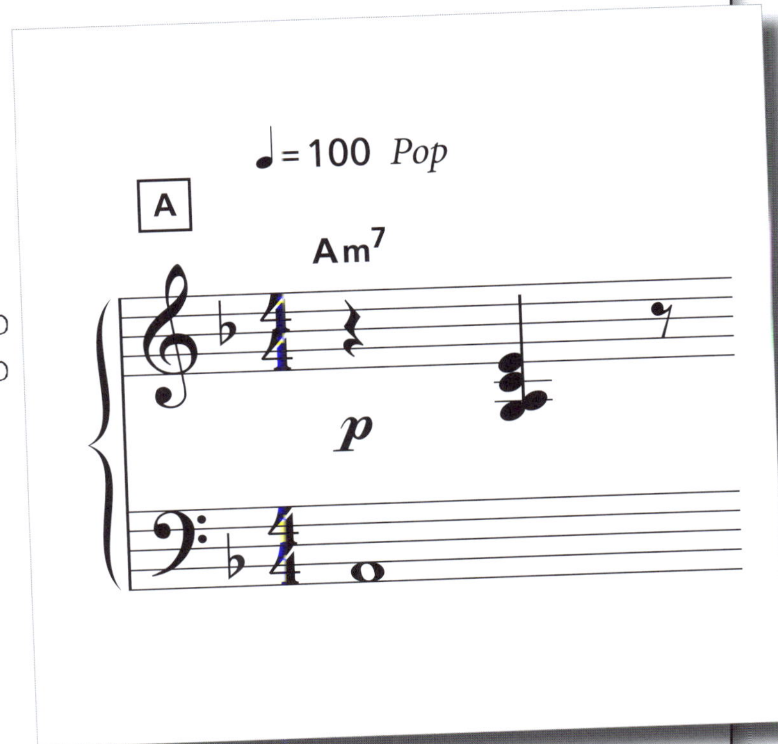

'Walk on By' was written for Dionne Warwick by Academy Award winners Burt Bacharach and Hal David. The song was written and recorded in 1963, but wasn't released until April 1964 when it peaked at number 6 in the US Billboard chart. The song was nominated for a Grammy in 1964 for Best Rhythm and Blues Recording, but lost out to Nancy Wilson's rendition of 'How Glad I Am'.

Warwick recorded the song at the same session which bore her hit 'Anyone Who Had a Heart', which hit the charts in January 1964 and landed her a top ten in the US, Canada, Spain, Netherlands, South Africa, Belgium and Australia. 'Walk on By' followed just four months later, topping the Cashbox R&B chart on its release. Billboard did not print rhythm and blues charts at this point, otherwise Warwick may well have had a Billboard number 1.

'Walk on By' was ranked 70 on the 'Rolling Stone' Magazine's list of The 500 Greatest Songs of all time, the second highest by a solo female artist on the list after Aretha Franklin's 'Respect'. It became Warwick's second worldwide million selling single, along with her previous hit 'Anyone Who Had a Heart'.

The song has since been covered on several occasions, often in wildly contrasting genres. The Stranglers 1978 punk rock rendition peaked at number 21 in the UK singles chart, delivering a completely different edge to the song. Artist Sybil released her adaption of the song in 1990 and achieved the hit's best UK chart position so far at number 6, followed closely by Gabrielle's 1997 version which peaked at number 7.

Burt Bacharach and Hal David hold four Academy Awards between them, they collaborated between the years of 1957 and 1973 and wrote hits for several global stars. Their most successful collaboration in the UK charts was 'Magic Moments', which they wrote for Perry Como and is famously known for its appearance in Nestle's advert for their family favourite – 'Quality Street'. The duo had international success with hits for artists such as Tom Jones, Dusty Springfield, Cilla Black and many more.

Dionne Warwick has won five Grammy awards throughout her career, with 14 nominations spanning from 1964 (her first for 'Walk on By') and 2013. She was awarded a Lifetime Achievement Award by both the Rhythm & Blues Foundation (2003) and the Women's World Awards (2004).

Walk On By

Dionne Warwick

Words by Hal David
Music by Burt Bacharach

2.
Fmaj7
Gm7
[19]
Am7
Gm7
Am7
[22]
Dm7
Am7
B♭maj7
[25]
B
C7
Fmaj7
B♭maj7♯11
f
[28]
Fmaj7
B♭maj7♯11
Fmaj7
[31]
B♭maj7♯11
Fmaj7
[34]

Notes

The melody to 'Walk On By' features pronounced, almost 'bouncing' syncopations which give contrast to the somewhat melancholy lyrical theme of the song. The syncopated rhythmic pattern of 'eighth note, quarter note, eighth note' (for example, in beats 3 and 4 of measure 4) can be found repeated throughout the piece, and this can be emphasised by keeping the first eighth note short and slightly accenting the off-beat quarter note, helping to bring life to the melody and providing a sense of momentum.

The song should begin quietly and maintain this volume throughout the first twelve measures. The *crescendo* through measures 13 to 15 needs to be controlled and help bring the music to a resounding *forte* at measure 15. This is the 'heartbreak moment'.

When moving to the second time ending in measure 21, be careful to keep the internal quarter-note pulse going so as to maintain a steady tempo throughout. Care will be needed to practise slowly in order to master the chorus parts (for example measures 13–20), which contain both the melody and the iconic piano riff in the right hand.

Students should ensure that the last F major 7 chord is held for the full two measures.

Technical Exercises

In this section you will be required to play a selection of exercises drawn from each of the groups below. The assessor will be looking for the speed of your response and will also give credit for the level of your musicality. Please see the syllabus guide for details on the marking criteria.

Major scales, minor scales and arpeggios need to be played hands together, in straight feel, ascending and descending, in the keys, octaves and tempos shown. Candidates can choose to play ***either*** natural minor ***or*** harmonic minor scales in the assessment. Pentatonic scales are right hand only, and the C blues scale needs to be performed hands separately. You may use your book for Group A and Group B. Group C exercises must be played from memory.

Note that Groups A and B need to be played to a click and any fingerings shown are suggestions only.

Group A: Scales
The tempo for this group is ♩= 66 bpm.

1. B♭ major scale

2. D major scale

3. G natural minor scale

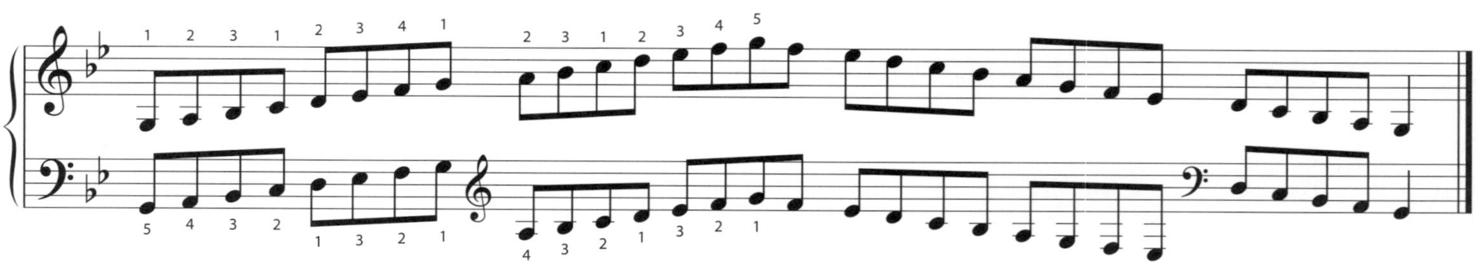

4. B natural minor scale

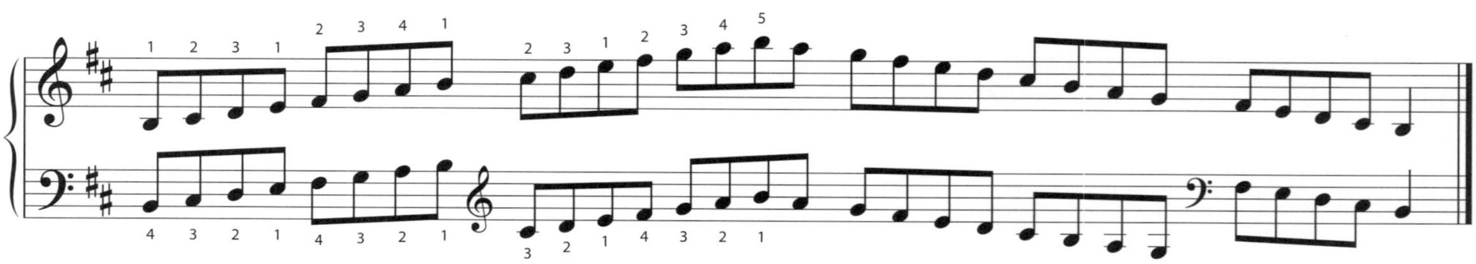

5. G harmonic minor scale

6. B harmonic minor scale

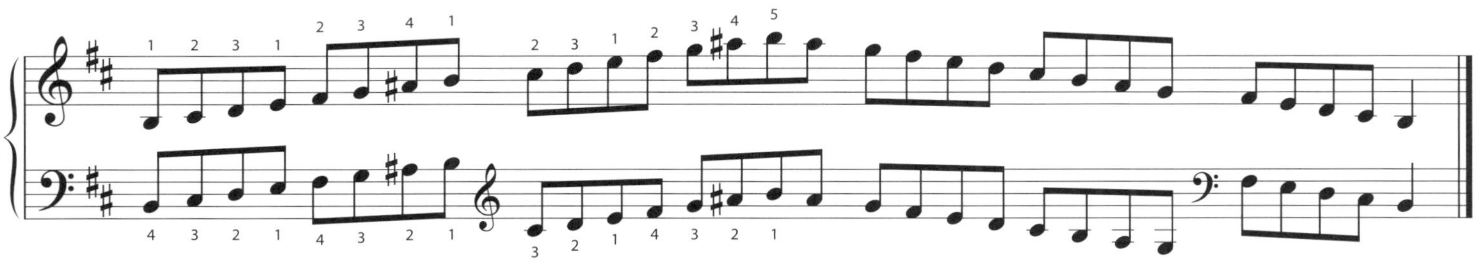

7. B♭ major pentatonic scale | right hand

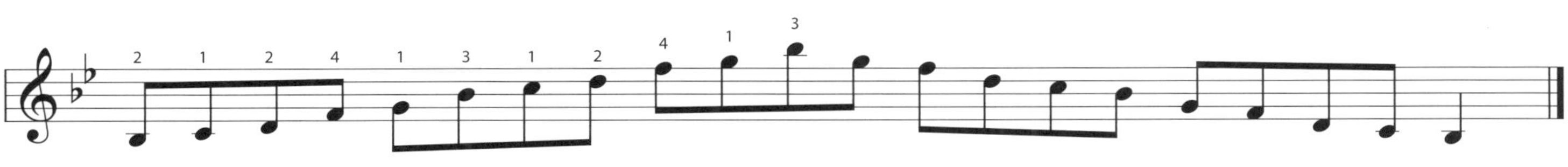

8. D major pentatonic scale | right hand

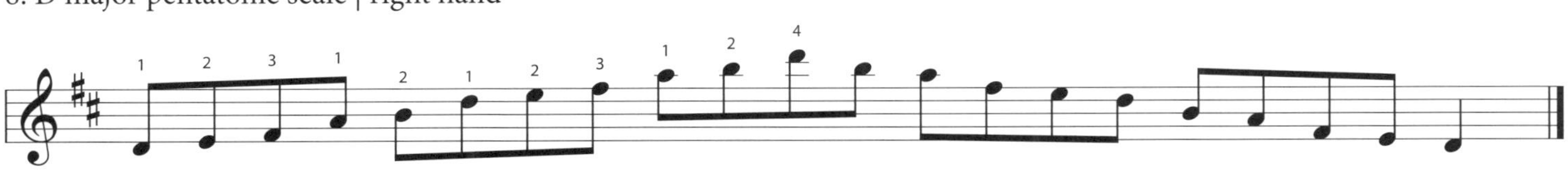

9. G minor pentatonic scale | right hand

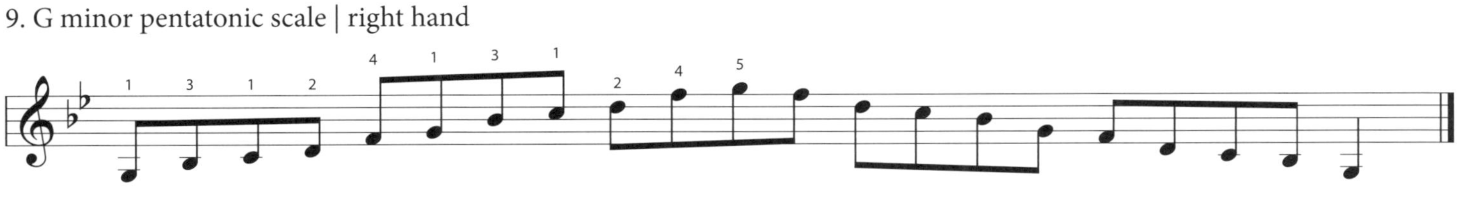

10. B minor pentatonic scale | right hand

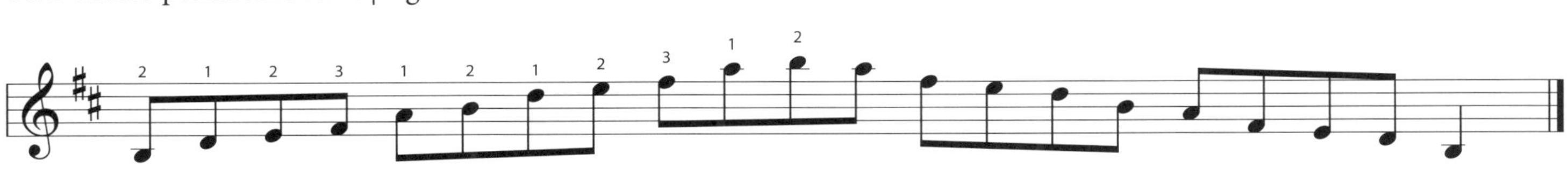

11. C blues scale | right hand

12. C blues scale | left hand

Group B: Arpeggios

The tempo for this group is ♩= 63 bpm.

1. B♭ major arpeggio

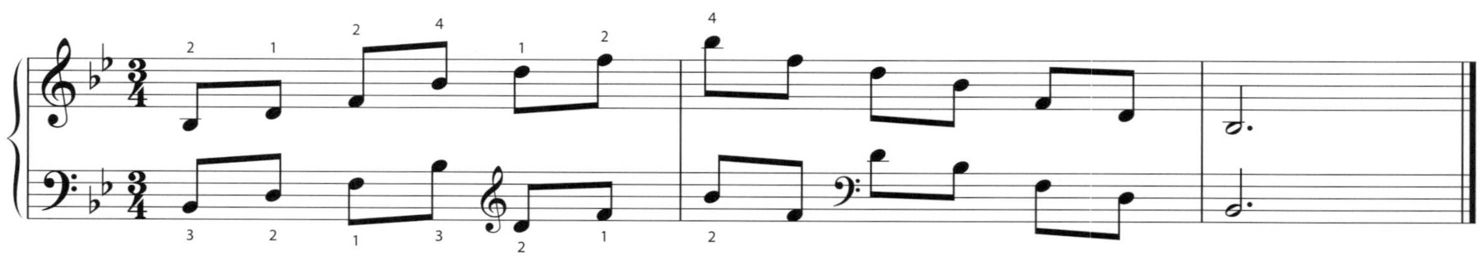

2. D major arpeggio

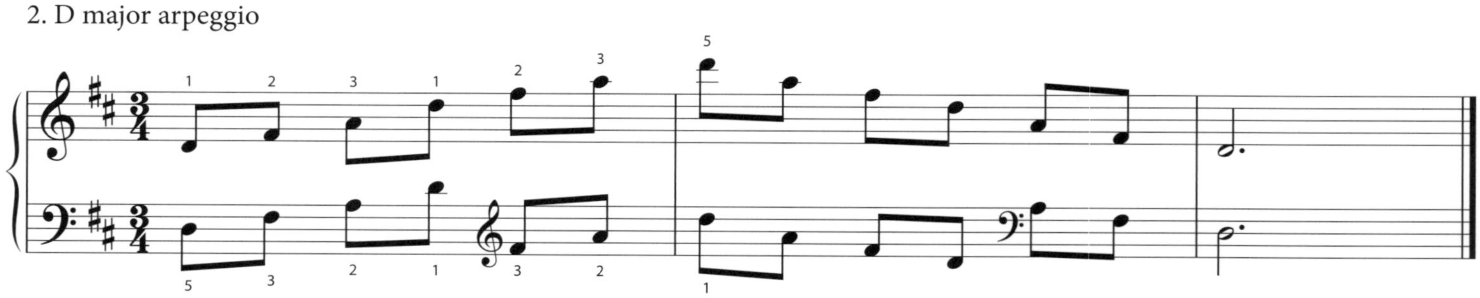

3. G minor arpeggio

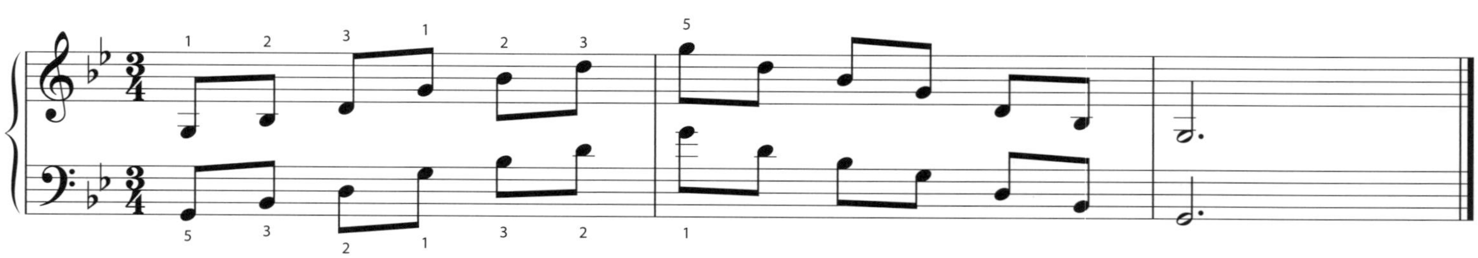

4. B minor arpeggio

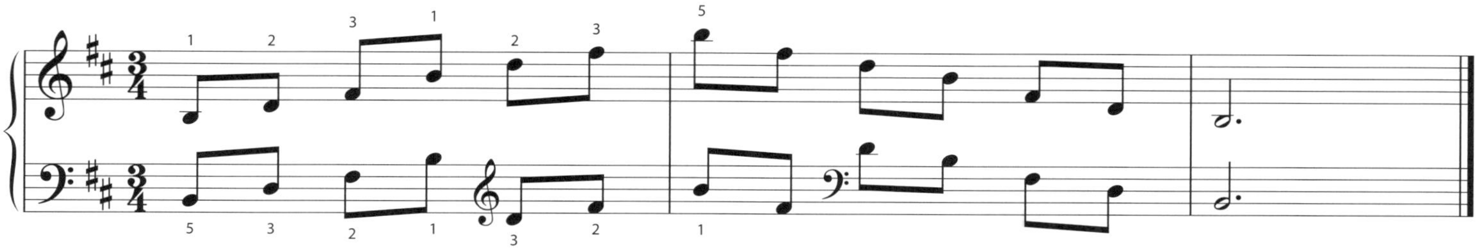

5. C major seventh (Cmaj^7) arpeggio

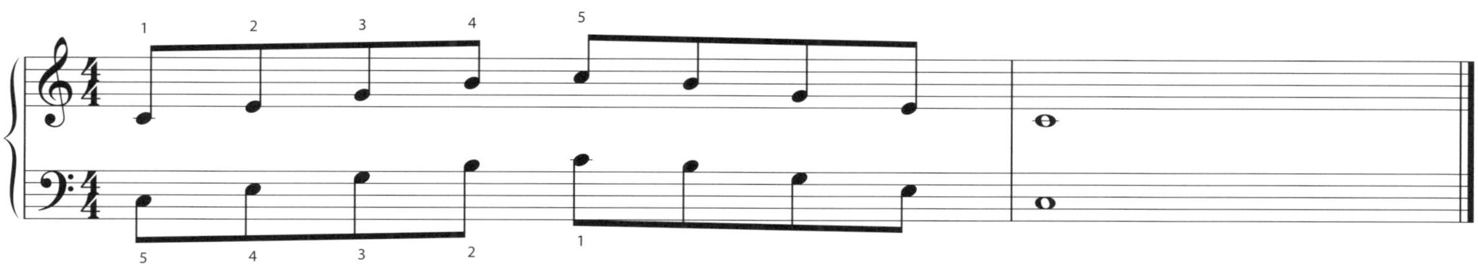

6. C minor seventh (Cm^7) arpeggio

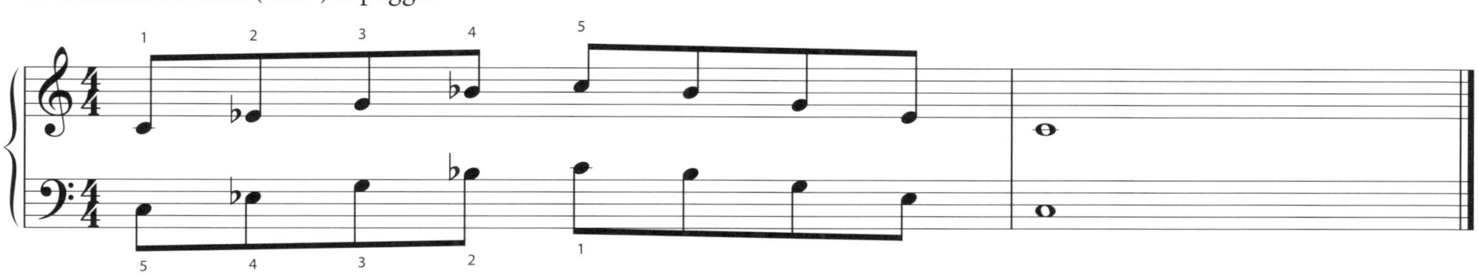

Group C: Chord Voicings

7th Chords

In the assessment you will be asked to play *one* of the 7th chord exercises below, from memory. This test is performed in free time (without backing track or click), but the assessor will be looking for the speed of your response.

Ex 1: Major 7th Chords

Ex 2: Minor 7th Chords

Ex 3: Dominant 7th Chords

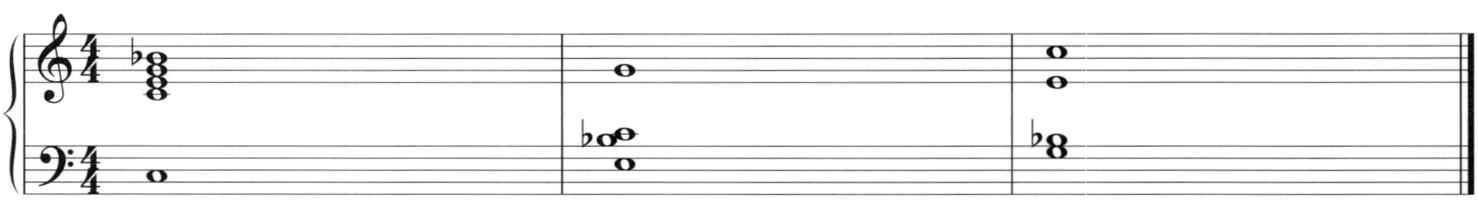

Sight Reading

In the assessment, you have a choice between either a Sight Reading test or an Improvisation & Interpretation test. The assessor will ask you which one you wish to choose before commencing. Once you have decided you cannot change your mind.

In the sight reading test, the assessor will give you a 4–6 measure melody in the key of either D major or B♭ major. You will first be given 90 seconds to practise, after which the assessor will play the backing track twice. The first time is for you to practise and the second time is for you to perform the final version for the assessment. For each playthrough, the backing track will begin with a one measure count-in. The tempo is ♩=60–95.

During the practice time, you will be given the choice of a metronome click throughout or a one measure count in at the beginning.

The backing track is continuous, so once the first playthrough has finished, the count in of the second playing will start immediately.

Sight Reading | Example 1

Please note: The test shown is an example. The assessor will give you a different version in the assessment.

Sight Reading | Example 2

Please note: The test shown is an example. The assessor will give you a different version in the assessment.

Improvisation & Interpretation

In the assessment, you have a choice between either a Sight Reading test or an Improvisation & Interpretation test. The assessor will ask you which one you wish to choose before commencing. Once you have decided you cannot change your mind.

In the Improvisation & Interpretation test, the assessor will give you a 4–6 measure chord progression in the key of either D major or B♭ major. You will first be given 90 seconds to practise, after which the assessor will play the backing track twice. The first time is for you to practise and the second time is for you to perform the final version for the assessment. For each playthrough, the backing track will begin with a one measure count-in. The tempo is ♩=60–95.

During the practice time, you will be given the choice of a metronome click throughout or a one measure count-in at the beginning.

The backing track is continuous, so once the first playthrough has finished, the count-in of the second playing will start immediately.

You are only required to improvise single note melodies, with either right or left hand. It is permissible to play chord voicings, but please note you will only be marked on melodic content.

Improvisation & Interpretation | Example 1

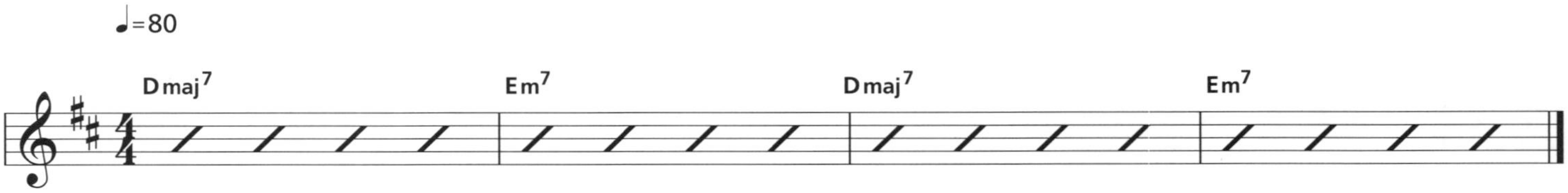

Please note: The test shown is an example. The assessor will give you a different version in the assessment.

Improvisation & Interpretation | Example 2

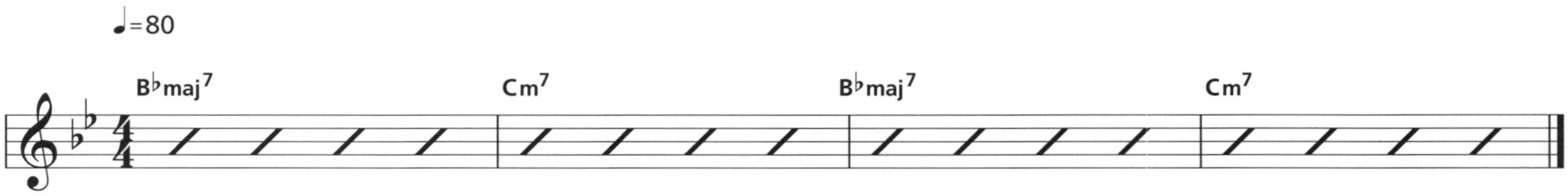

Please note: The test shown is an example. The assessor will give you a different version in the assessment.

Ear Tests

In this section, there are two ear tests:
- Melodic Recall
- Chord Recognition

You will find one example of each type of test printed below and you will need to perform both of them in the assessment.

Test 1: Melodic Recall

The assessor will play you a two measure diatonic melody in the key of C major with a range up to a fourth. The first note will be the root note. You will hear the test twice, each time with a one measure count-in, then you will hear a further one measure count-in after which you will need to play the melody to the click. The tempo is ♩=95 bpm.

It is acceptable to play over the track as it is being played as well as practising after the second playthrough. The length of time available after the second playthrough is pre-recorded on the audio track so the count-in may begin while you are still practising.

Please note: The test shown is an example. The assessor will give you a different version in the assessment.

Test 2: Chord Recognition

The assessor will play you a sequence of chords, each with a C root note. You will hear the chord sequence twice, each time with a one measure count-in. You will then be asked to identify the chord quality of each chord, from a choice of major, minor, diminished, augmented and dominant 7th. The tempo is ♩=95 bpm.

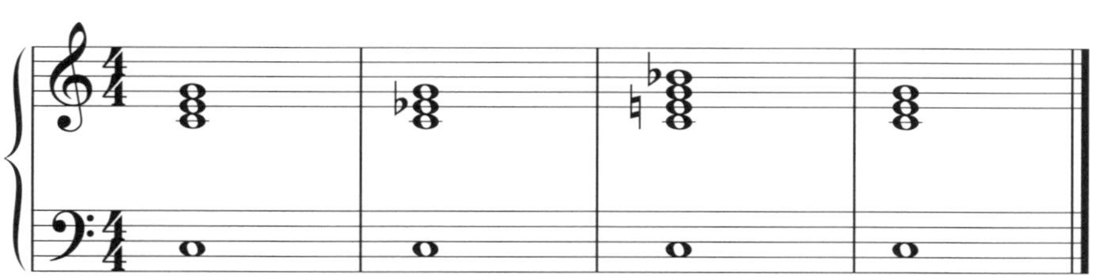

Please note: The test shown is an example. The assessor will give you a different version in the assessment.

General Musicianship Questions

The final part of your assessment is the General Musicianship Questions section, which features five questions relating to one of your choice of the performance pieces.

1. You will be asked a question relating to the harmony from a section of one of your pieces.
2. You will be asked a question relating to the melody in a section of one of your pieces.
3. You will be asked a question relating to the rhythms used in a section of one of your pieces.
4. You will be asked a question relating to the technical requirements of one of your pieces.
5. You will be asked a question relating to the genre of one of your pieces.

Further guidance on the types of questions asked at this level/grade can be found at the RSL website *www.rslawards.com*

Entering Rockschool Assessments

Entering a Rockschool assessment is easy, just go online and follow our simple six step process. All details for entering online, dates, fees, regulations and Free Choice pieces can be found at *www.rslawards.com*

- All candidates should ensure they bring their own Level/Grade syllabus book to the assessment or have proof of digital purchase ready to show the assessor.

- All Level/Grade 6–8 candidates must ensure that they bring valid photo ID to their assessment.

Marking Schemes

DEBUT TO LEVEL/GRADE 8

ELEMENT	PASS	MERIT	DISTINCTION
Performance Piece 1	12–14 out of 20	15–17 out of 20	18+ out of 20
Performance Piece 2	12–14 out of 20	15–17 out of 20	18+ out of 20
Performance Piece 3	12–14 out of 20	15–17 out of 20	18+ out of 20
Technical Exercises	9–10 out of 15	11–12 out of 15	13+ out of 15
Sight Reading *or* Improvisation & Interpretation	6 out of 10	7–8 out of 10	9+ out of 10
Ear Tests	6 out of 10	7–8 out of 10	9+ out of 10
General Musicianship Questions	3 out of 5	4 out of 5	5 out of 5
TOTAL MARKS	**60%+**	**74%+**	**90%+**

PERFORMANCE CERTIFICATES | DEBUT TO LEVEL/GRADE 8

ELEMENT	PASS	MERIT	DISTINCTION
Performance Piece 1	12–14 out of 20	15–17 out of 20	18+ out of 20
Performance Piece 2	12–14 out of 20	15–17 out of 20	18+ out of 20
Performance Piece 3	12–14 out of 20	15–17 out of 20	18+ out of 20
Performance Piece 4	12–14 out of 20	15–17 out of 20	18+ out of 20
Performance Piece 5	12–14 out of 20	15–17 out of 20	18+ out of 20
TOTAL MARKS	**60%+**	**75%+**	**90%+**

Copyright Information

Thinking Out Loud
(Sheeran/Wadge)
Sony/ATV Music Publishing (UK) Limited/BDi Music Limited

This Is Me (From "The Greatest Showman")
(Pasek/Paul)
EMI Music Publishing Limited (Twentieth Century Fox)/Kobalt Music Publishing

The Pink Panther Theme
(Mancini)
EMI United Partnership Limited

Feeling Good
(Bricusse/Newley)
Concord Music Limited

Roar
(Martin/Gottwald/McKee/Perry/Walter)
Kobalt Music Publishing Limited/Imagem Music /Warner/Chappell North America Limited

Walk On By
(David/Bacharach)
Warner/Chappell Music Publishing Limited/BMG Rights Management (US) LLC

mcps

Piano Notation Explained

THE MUSICAL STAVE shows pitches and rhythms and is divided by lines into measures. Pitches are named after the first seven letters of the alphabet.

Grace Note: Play the grace note on or before the beat depending on the style of music, then move quickly to the note it leads onto.

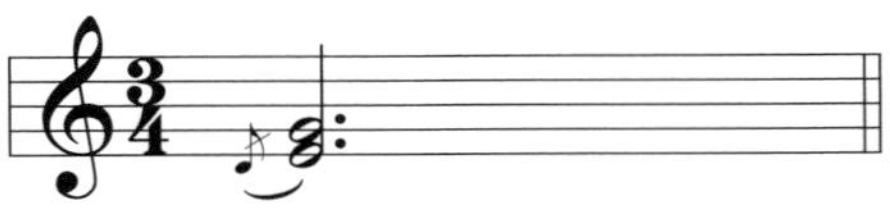

Pedal Marking: Depress and then release the sustain pedal. Multiple pedal operations in a short space of time may be simplified as shown in the last two beats of the measure below.

Spread Chord: Play the chord from the bottom note up (top down only if there is a downward arrow head). The final note should sound by the appropriate notated measure position.

Glissando: Play the notes between the notated pitches by sliding over the keyboard with the fingers or fingernails.

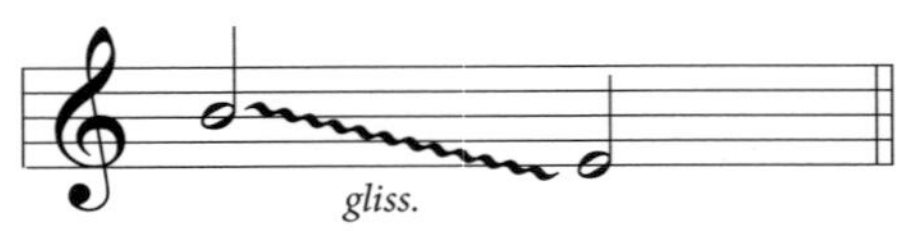

Tremolando: Oscillate at speed between marked notes.

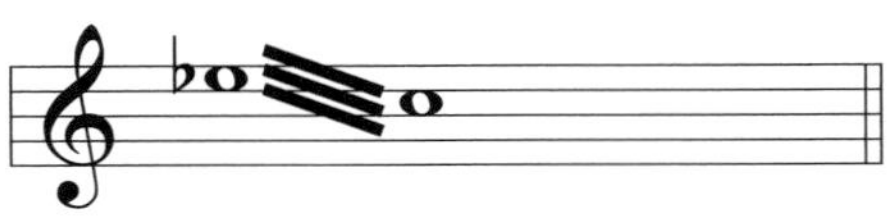

Finger Markings: These numbers represent your fingers. 1 is the thumb, 2 the index finger and so on.

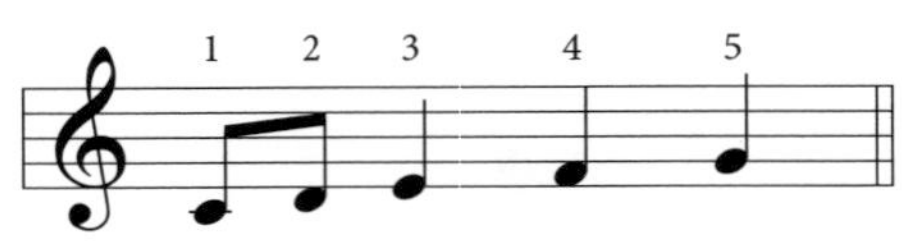

 (accent) • Accentuate note (play it louder).

 (accent) • Accentuate note with great intensity.

 (staccato) • Shorten time value of note.

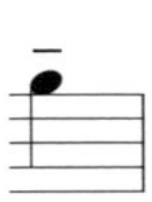 (accent) • Accentuate note with more arm weight.

D.𝄋. al Coda • Go back to the sign (𝄋), then play until the measure marked ***To Coda*** 𝄌 then skip to the section marked 𝄌 ***Coda***.

D.C. al Fine • Go back to the beginning of the song and play until the measure marked ***Fine*** (end).

Una Corda • Use soft pedal

 • Repeat the measures between the repeat signs.

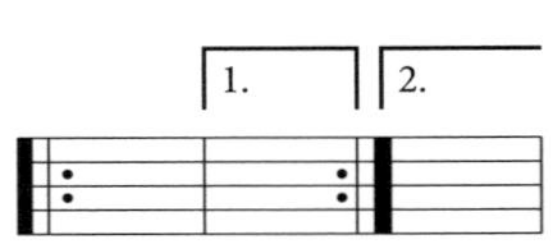

• When a repeated section has different endings, play the first ending only the first time and the second ending only the second time.